# Earthy
## Boho Jewelry

CW00762831

2

4

6

8

10

12

14

16

20

23

26

28

LEISURE ARTS, INC.
Maumelle, Arkansas

# Earth & Sky Earrings & Necklace

## SHOPPING LIST

- [ ] 20  6mm turquoise beads
- [ ] 6  6mm light mint faceted beads
- [ ] 6  6mm wood-look beads
- [ ] 8  3mm faceted gold metal beads
- [ ] 2  3mm copper spacers
- [ ] 10" length of antique copper very small link chain
- [ ] 2  antique copper crimp beads
- [ ] 3  15mm antique copper hoops
- [ ] 2  antique copper ball head pins
- [ ] 2  antique copper ear wires
- [ ] 2  4mm antique copper jump rings
- [ ] 2  7mm antique copper jump rings
- [ ] antique copper lobster clasp
- [ ] 24-gauge antique copper wire
- [ ] 49-strand/.018" bead stringing wire
- [ ] brown suede lacing
- [ ] crimp tool
- [ ] round-nose pliers
- [ ] chain-nose pliers (2 pair)
- [ ] wire cutters

*Be sure to read the **General Instructions** on pages 30-32 before making your project.*
*Necklace Finished Length: about 19", excluding tassel*

## To make each Earring:

1. Thread a turquoise bead, a copper spacer, and a gold bead on a head pin. Make a wrapped loop, attaching the head pin to a 15mm hoop.
2. Attach the earring to an ear wire.

## To make the Necklace:

1. Cut two 5" chain lengths. Attach the clasp to one end of one chain length with a 4mm jump ring. Attach a 7mm jump ring to one end of the remaining chain length with a 4mm jump ring.
2. Use a crimp bead to attach the free end of one chain length to a 12" stringing wire length. Thread a gold bead on the wire. Add six 6mm beads (mixing the turquoise, light mint, and wood-look beads as desired) and another gold bead. Continue adding the larger beads in groups of six, separated by a gold bead, until you have used all the beads. Use a crimp bead to attach the free end of the remaining chain length to the wire.
3. Cut three 6" suede lacing lengths. Thread the lengths through the remaining 15mm hoop and fold over, aligning the ends. Secure by wrapping with a 6" antique copper wire length. Attach the hoop to necklace center with the remaining 7mm jump ring.

# Daisy Fields Earrings & Necklace

## SHOPPING LIST

- [ ] 106  4mm cream beads
- [ ] 76  3mm green faceted beads
- [ ] 6  6mm wood-look beads
- [ ] 2  4mm antique copper ball beads
- [ ] 2  3mm antique copper ball beads
- [ ] 3mm green rondelle bead
- [ ] 19  4mm antique copper bead caps
- [ ] 2  3mm antique copper daisy spacers
- [ ] 3" length of antique copper very small link chain
- [ ] 2  10mm antique copper tags
- [ ] 9 antique copper ball head pins
- [ ] 2 antique copper ear wires
- [ ] 2  6mm antique copper jump rings
- [ ] 2  3mm antique copper jump rings
- [ ] 2 antique copper crimp beads
- [ ] 2 piece antique copper swirl clasp
- [ ] 49-strand/.018" bead stringing wire
- [ ] crimp tool
- [ ] round-nose pliers
- [ ] chain-nose pliers (2 pair)
- [ ] wire cutters
- [ ] bead tray (optional)

Be sure to read the **General Instructions** on pages 30-32 before making your project.
*Necklace Finished Length: about 32"*

## To make each Earring:

1. Cut a 1¹/₂" chain length. Attach an ear wire to one end of the chain.
2. Thread a wood-look bead on a head pin. Make a wrapped loop, attaching the head pin to the bottom link of the chain. Repeat with 2  3mm green faceted beads and 1 cream bead, evenly spacing the beads up the chain length.
3. Attach a tag to the chain with a 3mm jump ring.

## To make the Necklace:

1. Using a bead tray or a towel-lined baking sheet, lay the beads in the following order:
   - 20 cream beads
   - bead cap, wood-look bead, bead cap
   - 1 cream bead
   - 18 green beads
   - 2 beads caps–together, facing like this ( )
   
   Repeat this sequence 3 more times, then add 20 more cream beads.
2. Use a crimp bead to attach a 6mm jump ring to a 40" stringing wire length. Thread a 3mm ball bead, a 4mm ball bead, a daisy spacer and a bead cap on the wire. Add the beads you laid out in Step 1. Then add a bead cap, a daisy spacer, a 4mm ball bead and a 3mm ball bead. Use a crimp bead to attach the remaining 6mm jump ring to the wire.

3. For the bead dangle on the clasp, thread the green rondelle bead and a bead cap on a head pin. Make a wrapped loop.
4. Attach one clasp piece and the bead dangle to one jump ring on the necklace. Attach the remaining clasp piece to the other jump ring.

# Eclectic Necklace

## SHOPPING LIST

- ☐ 82 3mm antique brass ball beads
- ☐ 2 4mm antique brass ball beads
- ☐ assorted aqua, tan, brown, cream, and antique brass beads (about 30-35)
- ☐ 15 4mm antique copper spacers
- ☐ 10 4mm antique copper bead caps
- ☐ 2 15mm antique copper hoops
- ☐ 4 antique copper crimp beads
- ☐ 42" length of 1.5mm diameter round leather cord
- ☐ 24-gauge antique copper wire
- ☐ 49-strand/.018" bead stringing wire
- ☐ crimp tool
- ☐ chain-nose pliers
- ☐ wire cutters
- ☐ bead tray (optional)

Be sure to read the **General Instructions** on pages 30-32 before making your project.
*Necklace Finished Length: about 29"*

## To make the Necklace:

1. Cut two 21" cord lengths. Holding the lengths together and leaving $1/2$" tails, thread the cord lengths through a hoop and fold over *(Fig. 1)*. Tightly wrap an 8" length of 24-gauge wire around the folded cord 12-15 times *(Fig. 2)*. Pinch the wire down with the chain-nose pliers, tucking the wire ends down into the wraps. Trim any excess wire. Repeat with the remaining hoop on the opposite end of the cords.

**Fig. 1**

**Fig. 2**

2. Use a crimp bead to attach one hoop to a 12" stringing wire length. Thread 80 3mm antique copper ball beads on the wire. Use a crimp bead to attach the remaining hoop to the beaded wire length.

3. Using a bead tray or a towel-lined baking sheet, lay out the assorted beads, bead caps, and spacers in the desired order (about 8$\frac{1}{2}$" worth).

4. Use a crimp bead to attach a 14" stringing wire length to one hoop. Beginning and ending with the 3mm and 4mm antique brass ball beads, thread the assorted beads, bead caps, and spacers on the wire. Use a crimp bead to attach the beaded wire length to the remaining hoop.

# Arrowhead Earrings & Necklace

## SHOPPING LIST

- ☐ 1³/₄" long aqua arrowhead pendant
- ☐ 32 3mm x 5mm black rondelle beads
- ☐ 24 3mm x 5mm turquoise rondelle beads
- ☐ 14 3mmx 6mm white rondelle beads
- ☐ 2 3mm x 5mm rust rondelle beads
- ☐ 14 8mm faceted dark rust beads
- ☐ 6 10mm x 15mm flat oval turquoise beads
- ☐ 14 5mm x 7mm silver beads
- ☐ 2 3mm silver ball beads
- ☐ 2 3mm silver daisy spacers
- ☐ silver toggle clasp
- ☐ 2 antique brass head pins
- ☐ 2 antique brass eye pins
- ☐ 2 antique brass ear wires
- ☐ 4-ply brown wax linen cord
- ☐ straight pin
- ☐ round-nose pliers
- ☐ chain-nose pliers
- ☐ wire cutters
- ☐ bead tray (optional)

Be sure to read the **General Instructions** on pages 30-32 before making your project. *Necklace Finished Length: about 24", excluding pendant*

## To make each Earring:

1. Thread a flat oval turquoise bead on a head pin. Make a wrapped loop, attaching the head pin to an eye pin.
2. Thread a black rondelle bead, a white rondelle bead, a silver daisy spacer, and a rust rondelle bead on the eye pin. Make a wrapped loop, attaching the eye pin to an ear wire.

## To make the Necklace:

1. Using a bead tray or a towel-lined baking sheet, place the arrowhead pendant at the center front. Starting next to the arrowhead, lay the remaining beads in the following order for *each* side of the necklace:
   - 2 black rondelle beads, 1 dark rust bead, 1 black rondelle bead, 1 white rondelle bead, 1 black rondelle bead
   - 3 turquoise rondelle beads, 1 large silver bead, 1 dark rust bead
   - 1 black rondelle bead, 1 white rondelle bead, 1 black rondelle bead, 1 turquoise flat oval bead, 1 large silver bead, 1 dark rust bead
   - 1 black rondelle bead, 1 white rondelle bead, 1 black rondelle bead, 3 turquoise rondelle beads

- 1 large silver bead, 1 dark rust bead, 1 black rondelle bead, 1 white rondelle bead, 1 black rondelle bead, 1 large silver bead, 1 dark rust bead
- 1 black rondelle bead, 1 white rondelle bead, 1 black rondelle bead, 3 turquoise rondelle beads, 1 large silver bead, 1 dark rust bead
- 1 black rondelle bead, 1 white rondelle bead, 1 black rondelle bead, 1 turquoise flat oval bead, 1 large silver bead, 1 dark rust bead
- 1 black rondelle bead, 3 turquoise rondelle beads, 1 large silver bead, 1 silver ball bead

2. Cut a 66" cord length. Cut the end of the cord at an angle and twist it tightly to make a "needle" for threading; retrim and twist the end as needed.

3. Thread one cord end through one clasp piece; slide the clasp about 4" onto the cord. Spacing so the knots are close to, but not on top of each other, tie 3-4 overhand knots around the longer cord end. Squeeze the knots to "press" them into the wax cord to reduce bulk. Trim the tail close to the last knot.

4. Thread the first 6 beads onto the cord. Slide the first bead tight against the knot. Tie an overhand knot, tight against the bead (use a straight pin to tighten the knot). Slide the next bead against the knot; tie another knot. Continue sliding beads up and tying knots until all 6 beads have been knotted onto the cord. Repeat with the remaining beads and pendant, working in groups of 6-8 beads. End with a knot.

5. Repeat Step 3 to attach the remaining clasp piece to the free end of the cord.

# Tree of Life Earrings & Necklace

## SHOPPING LIST

- ☐ 1¹⁄₂" diameter antique brass tree of life pendant
- ☐ 15  6mm purple beads
- ☐ 4  6mm antique brass ball beads
- ☐ 2  3mm antique brass ball beads
- ☐ 16  5mm x 8mm turquoise rondelles
- ☐ 2  5mm x 8mm white rondelles
- ☐ 4  10mm antique brass filigree beads
- ☐ 4  10mm turquoise flat round beads
- ☐ 4mm turquoise bead
- ☐ 7¹⁄₂" length of antique brass medium link chain
- ☐ antique brass coin charm
- ☐ 4  10mm antique brass hoops
- ☐ 3  4mm antique brass jump rings
- ☐ 2 antique brass head pins
- ☐ 2 antique copper ball head pins
- ☐ 32 antique brass eye pins
- ☐ 4 antique copper eye pins
- ☐ 2 antique copper ear wires
- ☐ chain-nose pliers (2 pair)
- ☐ round-nose pliers
- ☐ wire cutters

Be sure to read the **General Instructions** on pages 30-32 before making your project.
*Necklace Finished Length: about 26", excluding pendant*

## To make each Earring:

1. Make a bead connector with 2 turquoise rondelle beads and an antique copper eye pin. Make a bead connector with a purple bead and an antique copper eye pin. Referring to the photo for placement, open the loops and join the connectors. Join the connectors to an ear wire.
2. Thread a 3mm ball bead on a ball head pin. Make a wrapped loop, attaching the head pin to the earring.

## To make the Necklace:

1. Use a 4mm jump ring to attach a 10mm hoop to each end of the chain length; set aside.
2. Use the antique brass eye pins to make 12 purple bead connectors, 6 turquoise rondelle bead connectors with 2 beads each, 4 filigree bead connectors, 4 turquoise flat round bead connectors, 4  6mm brass ball bead connectors, and 2 white rondelle bead connectors.
3. Referring to the photo for placement, open the loops and join the connectors, adding a 10mm hoop about halfway along on each side. Join the ends to the hoops on the chain ends and to the pendant.
4. Thread a purple bead on a head pin. Make a wrapped loop, attaching the head pin to the chain center. Repeat with a 4mm turquoise bead. Use a 4mm jump ring to attach the charm to the chain.

# Artisan Necklace

## SHOPPING LIST

- [ ] 29  4.5mm lime green beads
- [ ] 7" length of 8mm x 20mm elongated oval mauve pre-joined bead strand
- [ ] 22  8mm fuchsia beads
- [ ] 32  4mm antique brass ball beads
- [ ] 2  6mm antique brass ball beads
- [ ] 15" length of 5mm suede or leather lace
- [ ] 8" length of antique copper large link chain
- [ ] 2  15mm antique copper jump rings
- [ ] 6  5mm antique copper jump rings
- [ ] 2  4mm antique copper jump rings
- [ ] 2 antique copper fold-over cord ends
- [ ] 6 antique copper crimp beads
- [ ] 49-strand/.018" bead stringing wire
- [ ] craft glue
- [ ] crimp tool
- [ ] chain-nose pliers (2 pair)
- [ ] round-nose pliers
- [ ] wire cutters

Be sure to read the **General Instructions** on pages 30-32 before making your project.
*Necklace Finished Length: about 24"*

## To make the Necklace:

1. Lay one suede end in one fold-over cord end, apply a drop of glue, and use the chain-nose pliers to fold the tabs down over the suede end *(Fig. 1)*. Repeat with the opposite end of the suede.

**Fig.1**

2. Use a 5mm jump ring to connect a 15mm jump ring to each foldover cord end.
3. Use a crimp bead to attach a 12" wire length to a 15mm jump ring. Thread 30  4mm ball beads on the wire. Use a crimp bead to attach the wire to the remaining 15mm jump ring.
4. Use a crimp bead to attach a 12" wire length to a 15mm jump ring. Thread the lime green beads on the wire. Use a crimp bead to attach the wire to the remaining 15mm jump ring.
5. Use a 4mm jump ring to attach each end of the mauve bead length to a 15mm jump ring.

6. Use a crimp bead to attach a 12" wire length to a 15mm jump ring. Thread a 4mm brass ball bead, a 6mm brass ball bead, 22 fuchsia beads, the remaining 6mm brass ball bead, and the remaining 4mm brass ball bead on the wire. Use a crimp bead to attach the wire to the remaining 15mm jump ring.

7. Use two 5mm jump rings to attach each side of the chain length to a 15mm jump ring.

# Feather Earrings & Necklace

## SHOPPING LIST

- ☐ 2" long feather pendant
- ☐ 2  8mm x 10mm flat oval coral beads
- ☐ blue/grey fresh water pearl
- ☐ 11  3mm teal beads
- ☐ 2  8mm orange faceted beads
- ☐ 28" length of antique brass small link chain
- ☐ 2 antique brass connectors for earrings
- ☐ 3  15mm antique copper hoops
- ☐ 10mm antique copper circle tag
- ☐ 2  8mm antique copper bead caps
- ☐ 5mm antique copper jump ring
- ☐ 7  4mm antique copper jump rings
- ☐ 7 antique brass eye pins
- ☐ 3 antique brass head pins
- ☐ 2 antique brass ear wires
- ☐ antique brass hook and eye clasp
- ☐ round-nose pliers
- ☐ chain-nose pliers (2 pair)
- ☐ wire cutters

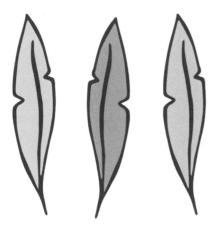

Be sure to read the General Instructions on pages 30-32 before making your project.
*Necklace Finished Length: about 23", excluding pendant*

## To make each Earring:

1. Attach one end of a brass connector to an ear wire.
2. Thread a bead cap and an orange bead on an eye pin. Make a wrapped loop, attaching the eye pin to the brass connector.
3. Thread a teal bead on a head pin. Make a wrapped loop, attaching the head pin to the earring.

## To make the Necklace:

1. Cut a 7" chain length and set aside.
2. From the remaining chain, cut:
   - two 4" lengths
   - one 3$^1/_2$" length
   - one 2" length
   - one 1$^1/_2$" length
   - two 1" lengths
   - one $^1/_2$" length
3. Use the eye pins to make 2 coral bead connectors, a pearl bead connector, and 2 teal bead connectors with 3 beads each.
4. Join a 4" and the 3$^1/_2$" chain length with a teal 3-bead connector. Use a 4mm jump ring to join a 15mm hoop to the free end of the 3$^1/_2$" chain length. Use a 4mm jump ring to join a 1" chain length to the 15mm hoop. Join the free end of the 1"chain length to a coral bead connector.

5.  Join the 2" chain length to the free end of the coral bead connector. Join the pearl bead connector to the free end of the 2" chain length and to the $1^{1}/_{2}$" chain length. Join the remaining teal 3 bead connector the free end of the $1^{1}/_{2}$" chain length and to the remaining 1" chain length. Join the remaining coral oval bead connector the free end of the $1^{1}/_{2}$" chain length and to the $^{1}/_{2}$" chain length.

6.  Use a 4mm jump ring to join the free end of the $^{1}/_{2}$" chain length to a 15mm hoop. Use a 4mm jump ring to join the 15mm hoop to the remaining 4" chain length.

7.  Join the clasp pieces to the free ends of the necklace.

8.  To make the pendant, use a 4mm jump ring to attach the feather to the remaining 15mm hoop. Thread 3 teal beads on a head pin. Make a wrapped loop, attaching the head pin to the hoop. Use the 5mm jump ring to attach the pendant to the necklace center.

9.  Use 4mm jump rings to attach the reserved 7" chain length to the necklace about $6^{1}/_{2}$" to 7" from each end of the necklace, adding the tag to one jump ring.

# Wild Child Earrings & Necklace

## SHOPPING LIST

- ☐ size 6/0 seed beads – dark brown, amber, mauve (about 355 of each color)
- ☐ 97  3mm bronze cube beads
- ☐ 2  6mm rust beads
- ☐ 6mm dark yellow bead
- ☐ 4  6mm antique brass ball beads
- ☐ 3  4mm antique brass ball beads
- ☐ 3mm x 5mm aqua rondelle bead
- ☐ 3mm copper spacer
- ☐ 3mm copper daisy spacer
- ☐ 1" long antique bronze cross charm
- ☐ antique bronze bird connector
- ☐ 2 large antique copper cones
- ☐ large antique brass lobster clasp
- ☐ 7mm antique brass jump ring
- ☐ 2  4mm antique copper jump rings
- ☐ 14  antique copper crimp beads
- ☐ 49-strand/.018" bead stringing wire
- ☐ 18-gauge antique copper wire
- ☐ 8 antique copper head pins
- ☐ 2 antique brass drop connectors
- ☐ 2 antique brass ear wires
- ☐ crimp tool
- ☐ round-nose pliers
- ☐ chain-nose pliers (2 pair)
- ☐ wire cutters

Be sure to read the **General Instructions** on pages 30-32 before making your project.
*Necklace Finished Length: about 26"*

## To make each Earring:

1. Thread a mauve seed bead on a head pin. Make a wrapped loop, attaching the head pin to the drop connector. Repeat with an amber bead and a brown bead.
2. Attach the drop connector to an ear wire.

## To make the Necklace:

1. Cut two 6" lengths of 18-gauge wire. Using the round nose pliers, create a large wrapped loop on one end of one wire length. Tighten the wraps with the chain-nose pliers. Repeat with the remaining wire length.
2. Use a crimp bead to attach an 18" stringing wire length to one wire loop *(Fig. 1)*.

Fig. 1

*Continued on page 18.*

# Wild Child Necklace continued

3. Thread beads on the stringing wire as follows:
   - 20 brown beads, then 2 cube beads; five times total
   - 10 brown beads and use a crimp bead to attach the cross charm to the wire. Use a crimp bead to attach a 12" wire length to the opposite end of the cross.
   - 10 brown beads, 2 cube beads
   - 20 brown beads, 2 cube beads; two times total
   - 10 brown beads

   Use a crimp bead to attach the stringing wire to the remaining wire loop.

4. Attach a 27" stringing wire length to a wire loop. Thread beads on the stringing wire as follows:
   - 20 brown beads, 2 cube beads
   - 10 brown beads, 6mm dark yellow bead, 10 brown beads, 2 cube beads
   - 20 brown beads, 2 cube beads; six times total
   - 10 brown beads

   Use a crimp bead to attach the stringing wire to the remaining wire loop.

5. Attach a 27" stringing wire length to a wire loop. Thread beads on the stringing wire as follows:
   - 20 amber beads, 2 cube beads; four times total
   - 10 amber beads, 6mm ball bead, 10 amber beads, 2 cube beads
   - 20 amber beads, 2 cube beads
   - 10 amber beads, 6mm rust bead, 10 amber beads, 2 cube beads
   - 20 amber beads, 2 cube beads, 20 amber beads

   Use a crimp bead to attach the stringing wire to the remaining wire loop.

6. Attach a 27" stringing wire length to a wire loop. Thread beads on the stringing wire as follows:
   - 5 amber beads, 2 cube beads
   - 10 amber beads, 6mm ball bead, 10 amber beads, 2 cube beads
   - 20 amber beads, 2 cube beads
   - 10 amber beads, 6mm rust bead, 10 amber beads, 2 cube beads
   - 20 amber beads, 2 cube beads; three times total
   - 10 amber beads, 6mm ball bead, 10 amber beads, 2 cube beads, 20 amber beads

   Use a crimp bead to attach the stringing wire to the remaining wire loop.

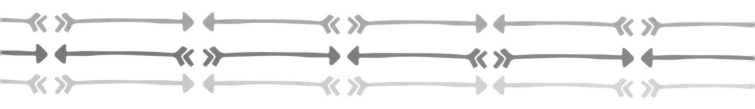

7. Attach a 27" stringing wire length to a wire loop. Thread beads on the stringing wire as follows:
   - 10 mauve beads, 2 cube beads
   - 20 mauve beads, 2 cube beads
   - 10 mauve beads, 6mm ball bead, 10 mauve beads, 2 cube beads
   - 20 mauve beads, 2 cube beads; five times total
   - 20 mauve beads

   Use a crimp bead to attach the stringing wire to the remaining wire loop.

8. Attach a 27" stringing wire length to a wire loop. Thread beads on the stringing wire as follows:
   - 20 mauve beads, 2 cube beads; eight times total
   - 20 mauve beads

   Use a crimp bead to attach the stringing wire to the remaining wire loop.

9. Thread one wire loop through a cone and gently pull until the beaded strands are seated nicely at the cone opening. Thread a 4mm ball bead on the wire and make a wrapped loop. Repeat with the remaining wire loop and cone.

10. Use a 4mm jump ring to attach the lobster clasp to one end of the necklace.

11. Thread the aqua bead, daisy spacer, and a 3mm ball bead on a head pin. Make a wrapped loop, attaching the head pin to the 7mm jump ring. Thread a mauve seed bead, copper spacer, and cube bead on a head pin. Make a wrapped loop, attaching the head pin to the tail of the bird connector. Use a 4mm jump ring to attach the bird connector to the 7mm jump ring. Attach the 7mm jump ring to the remaining end of the necklace.

# Midnight Desert Bracelet

## SHOPPING LIST

- ☐ size 6/0 amber seed beads (about 40-55)
- ☐ size 6/0 metallic gold seed beads (about 40-55)
- ☐ 4mm dark red faceted beads (about 30-40)
- ☐ 8mm orange faceted bead
- ☐ 12" length of antique brass small link chain
- ☐ 1¹⁄₂" length of antique brass large link chain
- ☐ 10" length of 2mm suede lace
- ☐ 2 large antique copper cones
- ☐ antique copper elephant charm
- ☐ 18-gauge antique copper wire
- ☐ 6 antique copper crimp beads
- ☐ 2 antique copper fold-over cord ends
- ☐ antique brass lobster clasp
- ☐ antique copper ball head pin
- ☐ 7  4mm antique copper jump rings
- ☐ 49-strand/.018" bead stringing wire
- ☐ crimp tool
- ☐ round-nose pliers
- ☐ chain-nose pliers (2 pair)
- ☐ wire cutters

Be sure to read the **General Instructions** on pages 30-32 before making your project.

**To make the Bracelet:**

1. Cut two 6" lengths of 18-gauge wire. Make a wrapped loop on one end of each wire length.
2. Use a crimp bead to attach a 12" stringing wire length to a wrapped wire loop *(Fig. 1)*. Thread the red beads on the wire until the beaded section is as long as your finished bracelet minus the length of the clasp and the 2 cones. Use a crimp bead to attach the beaded strand to the remaining wrapped wire loop.

**Fig. 1**

3. Repeat Step 2 with the amber seed beads and the metallic gold seed beads.

*Continued on page 22.*

# Midnight Desert Bracelet continued

4. Attach a fold-over cord end to one end of the suede lace *(Fig. 2)*. Trim the suede lace the same length as the beaded sections and attach the remaining cord end to the free end of the suede. Use jump rings to attach the cord ends to the wire loops.

**Fig. 2**

5. Cut three 1" lengths of the small link chain; set aside. Cut a piece of the small link chain the same length as the beaded sections and use jump rings to attach the chain to the wire loops.

6. Thread one wire loop through a cone and gently pull until the beaded strands, suede strand, and chain are seated nicely at the cone opening. Make a wrapped loop. Repeat with the remaining wire loop and cone, attaching the large link chain before you wrap the loop.

7. Thread the orange bead on the ball head pin. Make a wrapped loop, attaching the head pin to the free end of the large link chain. Use a jump ring to attach the charm to the chain.

8. Use a jump ring to attach the clasp to the remaining wire loop.

9. Use a jump ring to attach the 1" chain lengths to the wire loop on the clasp end of the bracelet.

# Harmonious Necklace

*Shown on page 25.*

## SHOPPING LIST

- ☐ 80 3mm antique brass ball beads
- ☐ assorted gold, red, turquoise, brown, green, orange, cream, black, and yellow beads (about 30-35)
- ☐ 4-ply brown wax linen cord
- ☐ 2 antique copper clam shell bead tips
- ☐ 2 4mm antique brass jump rings
- ☐ antique brass lobster clasp
- ☐ 1" length of antique brass large link chain
- ☐ antique copper ball head pin
- ☐ straight pin
- ☐ round-nose pliers
- ☐ chain-nose pliers (2 pair)
- ☐ wire cutters

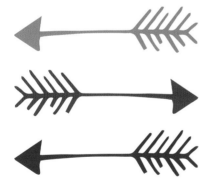

Be sure to read the **General Instructions** on pages 30-32 before making your project.
*Necklace Finished Length: about 22"*

## To make the Necklace:

1. Cut a 62" wax cord length. Cut the end of the cord at an angle and twist it tightly to make a "needle" for threading; retrim and twist end as needed.

2. Thread one cord end through the hole of a bead tip. Tie a few tight knots and trim the excess cord. With the knots in the clam shell, use the chain-nose pliers to gently press the bead tip closed, being careful not to bend the loop end *(Fig. 1)*.

**Fig. 1**

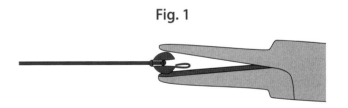

*Continued on page 24.*

# Harmonious Necklace continued

3. Tie an overhand knot close to the bead tip. Thread 10 ball beads onto the cord. Slide the first bead tight against the knot. Tie an overhand knot, tight against the bead (use a straight pin to tighten the knot). Slide the next bead against the knot; tie another knot. Continue sliding beads up and tying knots until all 10 beads have been knotted onto the cord. Repeat with the remaining ball beads, working in groups of 10, until you've used 40 ball beads. End with a knot.

4. Set a small colored bead aside. Tying a knot between each one, add the assorted beads to the cord until the beaded/knotted section is the same length as the ball bead section. End with a knot.

5. Tying a knot between each one, add 40 more ball beads to the cord. End with a knot.

6. Repeat Step 2 to attach the remaining bead tip to the free end of the cord.

7. Use a jump ring to attach the clasp to a bead tip.

8. Use a jump ring to attach the chain length to the remaining bead tip.

9. Thread the reserved bead on the head pin. Make a wrapped loop, attaching the head pin to the free end of the chain.

# Mesmerizing Earrings

## SHOPPING LIST

- [ ] 2 5mm x 8mm dark red rondelle beads
- [ ] 2 4mm antique copper daisy spacers
- [ ] 2 antique copper ear wires
- [ ] 13" length of antique copper very small link chain
- [ ] 20-gauge antique copper wire
- [ ] round-nose pliers
- [ ] chain-nose pliers (2 pair)
- [ ] wire cutters

Be sure to read the **General Instructions** on pages 30-32 before making your project.

### To make each Earring:

1. Cut three 2" chain lengths.
2. Cut a 2" wire length. Make a wrapped loop, attaching the chain lengths before wrapping.
3. Thread a bead and a spacer on the wire. Make a wrapped loop.
4. Attach the ear wire to the earring.

# Relics Bracelet

## SHOPPING LIST

- ☐ assorted aqua, tan, brown, cream, pearl, and gold beads (about 20-30)
- ☐ 3mm copper spacer
- ☐ 15mm antique copper hoop
- ☐ 4 10mm antique copper circle tags
- ☐ 7 4mm antique copper jump rings
- ☐ 7mm antique copper jump ring
- ☐ 10" length of antique brass large link chain
- ☐ antique brass lobster clasp
- ☐ 2 antique copper crimp beads
- ☐ antique copper ball head pin
- ☐ 49-strand/.018" bead stringing wire
- ☐ crimp tool
- ☐ chain-nose pliers (2 pair)
- ☐ round-nose pliers
- ☐ wire cutters

Be sure to read the **General Instructions** on pages 30-32 before making your project.

**To make the Bracelet:**

1. Use a crimp bead to attach a 12" wire length to the 15mm hoop. Setting aside 1 small bead, thread the assorted beads on the wire until the beaded area (including the hoop) is the desired finished length minus the clasp length. Use a crimp bead to attach the wire to the 7mm jump ring.

2. Cut a $5/8$" chain length and set aside. Use 4mm jump rings to attach the remaining chain to the hoop and the 7mm jump ring, trimming the excess chain as necessary.

3. Attach the short chain to the 7mm jump ring. Use 4mm jump rings to attach the tags to the chains as desired.

4. Thread the reserved small bead and copper spacer on the head pin. Make a wrapped loop, attaching the head pin to the free end of the chain. Use a 4mm jump ring to attach the clasp to the hoop.

# General Instructions

## TOOLS

**Chain-nose pliers** have rounded, tapered jaws and a flat interior surface that will not mar wire. These pliers are used for reaching into tight places, gripping objects, opening and closing jump rings, and bending wire.

**Round-nose pliers** have round jaws that are useful for making loops and bending wire smoothly.

**Wire cutters** are used to cut small gauge wire, head pins, and eye pins.

A **crimp tool** (also known as crimping pliers) flattens and shapes the crimp bead or crimp tube.

Chain-nose pliers

Round-nose pliers

Wire cutters

Crimp Tool

# TECHNIQUES

## Opening and Closing Loops, Chain Links, or Jump Rings

Hold one side of the loop, link, or jump ring with chain-nose pliers. With a second pair of chain-nose pliers, gently hold the other side of the loop. Open the loop by pulling one pair of pliers toward you while pushing the other away *(Fig. 1)*.

Close the loop by pushing and pulling the pliers in opposite directions, bringing the loop ends back together.

## Making Bead Dangles and Bead Connectors

To make a bead dangle, slide the bead(s) on a head pin. Leaving about $1/2$", cut off the excess wire. Using chain-nose pliers, bend the wire at a 90° angle *(Fig. 2)*. Grasp the wire end with the round-nose pliers. Turn the pliers and bend the wire into a loop *(Figs. 3-4)*. Release the pliers. Straighten or twist the loop further if necessary.

To make a bead connector, slide the bead(s) on an eye pin. Follow bead dangle instructions, above, to make a loop on the end of an eye pin.

Fig. 1    Fig. 2    Fig. 3    Fig. 4

## Making a Wrapped Loop on a Head Pin, Eye Pin, or Wire End

Slide the bead(s) on a head pin, eye pin, or wire end. Using chain-nose pliers, bend the wire at a 90° angle about $1/8$" above the bead *(Fig. 5)*. Grasp the wire with the round-nose pliers at the 90° bend. Use your finger to push the wire around the barrel of the pliers *(Fig. 6)*. Remove the pliers. Now is the time to slide the loop onto your project or to add something to the wrapped loop. Holding the loop with the chain-nose pliers, use a second pair of chain-nose pliers to wrap the wire end around itself above the bead 3-5 times *(Fig. 7)*. Trim the excess wire and tuck the wire end into the wraps with chain-nose pliers.

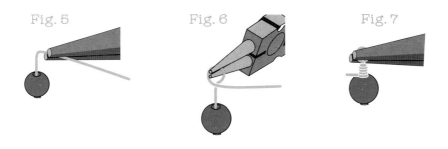

Fig. 5    Fig. 6    Fig. 7

## Using Crimp Beads

To finish a wire end, thread a crimp bead and the clasp or jump ring on the wire. Run the wire back through the crimp bead; use a pair of chain-nose pliers to pull and tighten the wire *(Fig. 8)*. Place the crimp bead on the inner groove of the crimp tool and squeeze *(Fig. 9)*.

Fig. 8

Pull to tighten

Fig. 9

Release the tool, turn the crimp bead a quarter turn, and place it in the outer groove *(Fig. 10)*. Squeeze the tool to round out the crimp bead *(Fig. 11)*. Trim the wire end or if the design calls for beads, thread the beads over the wire to cover the end.

Fig. 10

Fig. 11

## Tying Knots Between Beads

As you tie an overhand knot, slip a straight pin in the knot loop and guide the knot as close to the bead as possible *(Fig. 12)* near one end.

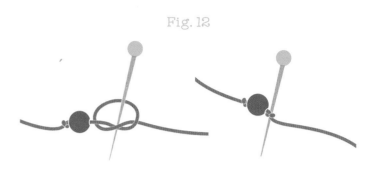

Fig. 12

Holly Witt-Allen would like to thank Blue Moon Beads, Beaducation, Hip Chickee Beads (found on etsy.com), Beadalon, and Vintaj Natural Brass Co. for providing some of the products used for her jewelry designs.

Production Team: Technical Writer – Mary Sullivan Hutcheson; Technical Associate – Jean Lewis; Editorial Writer – Susan Frantz Wiles; Senior Graphic Artist – Lora Puls; Graphic Artist – Cailen Cochran; Photostylist – Lori Wenger; Photographer – Jason Masters.